BOOK ANALYSIS

Written by Isabelle Consiglio and Lucile Lhoste
Translated by Rebecca Neal

The Marriage of Figaro

BY BEAUMARCHAIS

PIERRE BEAUMARCHAIS

FRENCH PLAYWRIGHT, POET, POLITICIAN AND MUSICIAN

- **Born in Paris in 1732.**
- **Died in Paris in 1799.**
- **Notable works:**
  - *Eugénie* (1767), play
  - *The Barber of Seville* (1775), play
  - *The Guilty Mother* (1792), play

Pierre-Augustin Caron was born in 1732 and is best known by the surname he later adopted, Beaumarchais, which is derived from "le Bois Marchais", an area of land that belonged to his wife. He initially followed in the professional footsteps of his father, who was a master watchmaker, before entering Parisian high society in 1759 as a music tutor for the daughters of King Louis XV (1710-1774). He gained a reputation as an incorrigible womaniser during this time, before being made Secretary-Councillor to the King, a position which saw him take on a number of diplomatic responsibilities.

Beaumarchais' first real taste of literary success came in 1775, when his play *The Barber of Seville* was first performed. After falling victim to censorship and the outdated practices of the Comédie-Française (a prestigious French state theatre), in 1777 he founded the *Société des auteurs dramatiques* ("Society of Playwrights"), which is generally considered to be the origin of the modern idea of copyright. Beaumarchais died in 1799.

THE MARRIAGE OF FIGARO

A THOUGHT-PROVOKING WORK OF SOCIAL CRITICISM

- **Genre:** play (comedy)
- **Reference edition:** Beaumarchais, P-A. (1964) *The Barber of Seville and The Marriage of Figaro*. Trans. Wood, J. London: Penguin.
- **1st edition:** 1784
- **Themes:** nobility, seduction, privilege, fidelity, social class, politics

The five-act prose comedy *The Madness of a Day, or the Marriage of Figaro*, more commonly known simply as *The Marriage of Figaro*, was first performed in 1784 and is the sequel to *The Barber of Seville* (1775). It is set in Spain, at the residence owned by Count Almaviva. In *The Barber of Seville*, Almaviva had sought his valet Figaro's help to marry Rosine, who was engaged to the elderly doctor Bartholo. Now, Figaro wants to marry Rosine's maid Suzanne, but Almaviva is staunchly opposed to this union and does every-thing in his power to try and stop it.

Figaro's irreverent, provocative treatment of his aristocratic master makes *The Marriage of Figaro* a strikingly political play which foreshadowed the advent of the French Revolution in 1789.

SUMMARY

Preparations for Figaro's wedding are underway. He is set to marry Suzanne who, like him, works for Count Almaviva. Suzanne tells Figaro that Almaviva has made repeated advances towards her in an attempt to assert his *droit de seigneur*, a controversial feudal right (it allegedly allowed feudal lords to have sex with their female vassals on their wedding nights, but its existence has been called into question by scholars). Figaro therefore needs to find a way out of this situation.

This is not the only complication that Figaro is facing: he also owes a sizeable sum of money to Marceline, whose advances he previously rejected. Marceline asks the doctor Bartholo for his help and tries to use the debt to have Figaro's wedding called off. Furthermore, Almaviva postpones the wedding, claiming that he needs more time to prepare the ceremony; in reality, he is still trying to persuade Suzanne to sleep with him. When he becomes convinced that his page Chérubin is courting her, he offers him a distant army posting to get him far away from her.

ACT TWO

In reality, Chérubin is courting Rosine, not Suzanne. With Rosine's consent and help, Figaro plans to take his revenge on the Count by setting a trap for him: he gives Bazile, the Countess's music teacher, an anonymous letter addressed to her from a suitor who wants to meet her at a ball held that evening. The aim of this trick is to stoke Almaviva's jealousy and distract him from the upcoming wedding. Figaro also wants to get Chérubin (who only pretended to leave with the army) to dress up in Suzanne's clothes and attend a night-time assignation with Rosine.

When Chérubin is still in Rosine's apartment, Almaviva, who has flown into a jealous rage after reading the note addressed to his wife, tries to break the door down. The young page rushes into her powder room, and in the ensuing altercation he manages to throw himself out of the window just in time. Suzanne takes his place and Rosine manages to smooth things over, admonishing the Count for his failure to trust her and threatening to retire to a convent.

The Count's jealousy almost gets the better of him when the gardener tells him that he saw a man fall from an open window. Figaro now has to use all his cunning to convince the Count that the man was him and not Chérubin. Just as things seem to be back on track for the future spouses, Marceline arrives and claims that Figaro has to marry her because he did not pay back his debt to her.

ACT THREE

The first direct confrontation between Figaro and Almaviva takes place, as the Count is not convinced that the man who fell from the window was really his valet.

A few hours later, the legal proceedings between Figaro and Marceline begin at the castle. It is claimed that Figaro previously promised to marry Marceline if he did not return the money she had lent him. This leads to a debate between Figaro, who is defending himself, and Marceline's lawyer Bartholo. As the document setting out the loan is no longer legible, the court does not know whether Figaro is obligated to reimburse and marry Marceline, or if the marriage is compensation in the event that he does not pay back his debt.

Figaro claims that, since he is an orphan, he cannot secure his parents' consent and therefore cannot marry. Marceline then recognises the scar on his left arm and realises that he is in fact the son she had with Bartholo. Rosine offers Suzanne the dowry, which means that the wedding can take place immediately.

ACT FOUR

Now that everything finally seems to be ready for Suzanne and Figaro's wedding, the Countess helps to arrange a meeting between Suzanne and Almaviva with the aim of setting a trap for the jealous Count.

A second wedding is being organised at the castle, this time between Bartholo and Marceline. They had signed a promise many years earlier agreeing that if Marceline found the child that bandits had kidnapped from her, they would get married.

ACT FIVE

Figaro learns that Suzanne has agreed to a night-time assignation with the Count. He is plunged into despair and delivers a long monologue on female fidelity and the privileges of birth. When he sees Suzanne arriving, he hides in the park. In reality, the woman is the Countess, who has dressed up as her maid in order to trick her husband. Almaviva arrives and thinks that he is charming Suzanne; unbeknownst to him, he is offering a dowry and a diamond to his own wife. Meanwhile, Chérubin is flirting with Suzanne in the mistaken belief that she is the Countess. The Count then realises that a trick is being played on him, and Suzanne and Figaro's wedding takes place with an additional dowry.

CHARACTER STUDY

FIGARO

After being kidnapped by bandits as a child, Figaro was left with no real Christian name and no noble titles, and he claims that he tried his hand at every profession imaginable before working as a barber in Seville. This is where he met Count Almaviva; he went on to become the Count's valet and helped him to save Rosine from Bartholo's clutches.

Figaro's defining characteristic is his cunning: he is the archetypal valet who uses disguises and lies to deceive his master. He refuses to abide by the rigid social conventions of his time and his remarkable frankness sometimes borders on insolence when he is talking to aristocrats or lawyers.

He is madly in love with Suzanne and is prepared to do anything to prevent Count Almaviva from seducing her. He is well aware of the limitations placed on him by his social position and rebels against it through language rather than overt violence. Indeed, his countless provocative responses stem from his desperation at the place he occupies within society.

He is the central character of the play, which is structured by his unexpected appearances. He addresses the audience directly in numerous asides, which serve to foster sympathy for him.

SUZANNE

Suzanne is a young maid who is completely devoted to the Countess, and her directness makes her Figaro's female counterpart. She is determined and sardonic by nature, especially in her interactions with men. Differences in social class mean nothing to her, and she joins forces with Rosine to use disguises to trick Almaviva.

Her actions in the play are exhilarating, comical and dynamic. She is one of the few female characters in the Comédie-Française's repertoire who is not a naïve ingénue led into a trap by a wily seducer; on the contrary, she is cunning and jealous in her relationship with Figaro.

COUNT ALMAVIVA

The Count is a powerful man and the owner of the castle of Aguas-Frescas. He is cunning, sardonic, jealous and suspicious. He will stop at nothing to get what he wants and tries to abuse his position to force Suzanne to sleep with him. Indeed, even his wife describes him as a "tyrant". He is an inveterate womaniser, but struggles to deal with defeat or any kind of opposition to his plans. In this sense, he can be seen as a representation of the authority and rigid principles of men under the Ancien Régime (the social system in France prior to the French Revolution, 1515-1789).

It is interesting to consider how Almaviva evolves as a character: even though Figaro made his marriage to Rosine possible, he does not seem to feel any gratitude towards his valet and spends the entire play trying to seduce his fiancée. It is only after he realises that he has been tricked that he is forced to let Figaro and Suzanne marry.

COUNTESS ROSINE

Rosine is the only character in the play who has broken social barriers, as she has risen from non-aristocratic beginnings to become a countess. However, she has not forgotten her roots: in choosing to help Suzanne, she deceives her husband and clearly opposes his principles. She is generous and cheerful by nature, and shows her frivolous side when she flirts with Chérubin.

She is fully aware of her husband's intentions towards Suzanne and is critical of men in general. Although she is married, she demonstrates initiative and independence, and decides to deceive her husband in order to win him back and prove her worth to him.

MARCELINE

Marceline initially appears to be a secondary character, but as the play progresses she assumes an increasingly important role in the plot, leading up to the stunning revelation that she is actually Figaro's mother. Her priorities also change: at the start of the play, she is determined to get back the money she is owed or marry Figaro, in this way positioning herself as a rival to Suzanne, but later on she steps into the role of a protective mother and helps to make sure that the wedding takes place.

This character also serves to introduce the theme of women's position in society, as she is overtly critical of men and their often-selfish behaviour: for example, Bartholo fathered a child with her but then refused to marry her.

CHÉRUBIN

The Count's teenaged page Chérubin is in love with the Countess. He is hopelessly devoted to her, even going so far as to say that he would rather die than cause her harm: "[I'd throw myself] [i]nto the flaming pit itself [...] rather than any harm should come to her" (Act 2, Scene XIV). In fact, his expressions of love are so exaggerated that they verge on parody.

He takes great risks to see Rosine, and is almost caught in Act 2 (he is saved by Figaro, who pretends that he was visiting the Countess). He is unwittingly drawn into the final plot and finds himself flirting with Suzanne, as he thinks that she is Rosine, which serves to make him look ridiculous.

BARTHOLO

Bartholo, an elderly doctor from Seville, has a less important role in this play than in *The Barber of Seville*, in which he was determined to marry Rosine. He is reminiscent of the elderly men of classical comedies, as he is avaricious and quick-tempered, and is trying to attract a much younger woman.

In *The Marriage of Figaro*, he serves as Marceline's lawyer in her legal proceedings against Figaro. He also refuses to acknowledge that Figaro is his son.

ANALYSIS

Provocative content

The Marriage of Figaro was an immediate success, partly due to its light, dynamic tone and Figaro's repartee. However, the play also owes its success to its controversial ideas and political content. Indeed, the plot centres on a valet who defies his master when the latter tries to abuse the privileges afforded to him by his social position. In spite of the play's ostensibly light-hearted comic tone, its critical dimension is unmistakeable.

Royal censorship

Beaumarchais was concerned that his play might be too subversive, and his fears turned out to be justified: King Louis XVI (1754-1793) ordered it to be censored because he deemed it too critical of respected people and organisations. Although the author tried to present his play as a humorous love story, he could not prevent it from being interpreted as more critical, especially given that he wrote in his preface that the role of theatre was to expose the hidden vices and abuses of those in positions of power.

In *The Marriage of Figaro*, Beaumarchais is more critical of the Ancien Regime and its customs than in *The Barber of Seville*. Almaviva can be seen as a representation of the omnipotent absolute monarchy, given that his wife and servants have no choice but to obey him. For example, when he suspects that Chérubin is the Countess's lover, he threatens to send him far away. However, in spite of his power, he is unable to win over Suzanne. His desire to seduce her proves to be his downfall: Figaro, Suzanne and Rosine are aware of his weakness and use it to set a trap which makes him look ridiculous, as when he thinks he is courting Suzanne, he is actually flirting with his own wife. This means that the character who represents power within the play inspires laughter rather than admiration.

When the play was first performed, the ideas that it was able to express were limited by censorship. For example, the monarchy was riled by Beaumarchais' criticism of the omnipotence and unearned privileges enjoyed by the most powerful members of society, and by his criticism of the justice system, which is made to seem ridiculous in the legal case between Marceline and Figaro. The play is also very critical of politics, with Figaro claiming that it is nothing more than scheming and deceit.:

> "[T]o play a part well or badly, to encourage spies and reward traitors, to tamper with seals, intercept letters, and endeavour to compensate for poverty of means by exaggerating the importance of one's ends – that's all there is in politics or I'm sadly mistaken." (Act 3, Scene V)

A harbinger of the French Revolution?

The play's impact can be seen in the fact that two towering political figures, namely Georges Danton (French lawyer and politician, 1759-1794) and Napoleon Bonaparte (French general, first consul and emperor of the French, 1769-1821), both believed that Figaro's actions foreshadowed the French Revolution. The plot involves numerous role reversals: Figaro stands up to his master; women refuse to bow to the expectations of obedience that are placed on them; and servants rebel against the power that governs their lives when it stops them from getting what they want.

Beaumarchais also criticises the unearned privileges at the root of social inequality. In the feudal system which prevailed until 1789, society was based on feudal privileges (particular laws that applied to certain sectors of society, to the exclusion of everyone else), which were supposed to be guaranteed by the king. The resulting inequalities are shown in the play by the fact that the Count makes the rules, and everyone else has no choice but to obey him. It is much more difficult for Rosine and the servants to get what they want, no matter how hard they try:

> "Nobility, fortune, rank, position! How proud they make a man feel! What have *you* done to deserve such advantages? Put yourself to the trouble of being born – nothing more! For the rest – a very ordinary man! Whereas I, lost among the obscure crowd, have had to deploy more knowledge, more calculation and skill merely to survive than has sufficed to rule all the provinces of Spain for a century! Yet you would measure yourself against me..." (Act 5, Scene I)

This injustice makes for fertile ground for rebellion, and before long the servants start to fight for the right to make their own decisions. They no longer want to employ so much ingenuity for so little reward, and after Figaro uses his cunning to lead the rebellion, unearned privileges are abolished for a time.

Some authors and critics have seen Beaumarchais' socially conscious writing as a harbinger, or even the cause, of the French Revolution. Although this is perhaps a bold claim to make, it is undeniable that *The Marriage of Figaro* reflects the same political climate that gave rise to the Revolution.

REVITALISING COMIC THEATRE

In his theoretical writing on the theatre, Beaumarchais argued that the genre needed to change to become more fluid and expressive. He described *The Marriage of Figaro* as a serious play because it combines both tragic and comic elements. It contains a number of the classic features of comedy and farce, including:

- the master-servant pairing, with a servant who is more cunning than his master;
- characters disguising themselves or hiding in locations such as wardrobes;
- confusing situations or altercations between the characters;
- a dramatic plot twist and the discovery of a lost child;
- lower-status characters flouting the authority of their masters or elders.

However, the play also contains a number of innovative elements. Unlike in *The Barber of Seville*, the master and valet are no longer on the same side; rather, they are romantic rivals. Furthermore, the valet enjoys a remarkable degree of freedom of expression, openly criticising the nobility and its privileges, as well as the legal system. This means that Figaro's role is not just to entertain the audience: he is the mouthpiece through which a host of social demands are expressed.

Finally, the play's female characters are particularly strong and independent, and they reflect on the position of women in society and the concept of faithfulness.

THE RELATIONSHIP BETWEEN *THE MARRIAGE OF FIGARO* AND *THE BARBER OF SEVILLE*

In chronological terms, *The Marriage of Figaro* is set some time after *The Barber of Seville*. In *The Barber of Seville*, Almaviva courts Rosine, who at this stage is a commoner, an orphan and Bartholo's ward. Figaro, who is already Almaviva's valet in the first play, helps to ensure that the marriage can take place.

Almaviva, Figaro, Rosine and Bartholo all appear again in the second play, accompanied by new characters such as Marceline (who did not appear but was referred to in *The Barber of Seville*), Suzanne and Chérubin. These additions serve a dual purpose: firstly, they justify the new plot (Marceline plays a role in the final revelation, Suzanne is Figaro's fiancée and the object of Almaviva's attentions until the final act, and Chérubin unwittingly participates in the final misunderstanding); and secondly, they enable Beaumarchais to introduce new themes and relationships between his characters.

COMIC TECHNIQUES IN *THE MARRIAGE OF FIGARO*

Beaumarchais uses a number of techniques to make his audience laugh, including the creation of incongruous situations and the amusing plot twists. In particular, the play features:

- **Repetition.** This can be visual (for example, Suzanne and Marceline curtsey repeatedly when they are arguing in front of Bartholo in Act 1, Scene V) or verbal (for example, in Act 5, Scene XVIII, the Count repeatedly says "No, no" while the other characters kneel in front of him).
- **Inversion.** As its name suggests, inversion works by reversing the initial situation. In Act 5, Scene VIII, Figaro believes that Suzanne is being unfaithful to him, unaware that she and Rosine have each disguised themselves as the other in order to lay a trap for Almaviva. He realises what is happening while he is alone with Suzanne (disguised as Rosine), but he does not let on that he knows and turns her attempts at seduction against her:

"FIGARO [with a comic pretence of emotion]: Ah, Madam, I adore you! Consider the time and the place and the circumstances – and may your resentment make up for any graces my supplications may lack!

SUZANNE [aside]: My hand is itching!

FIGARO [aside]: My heart is pounding!"

When Suzanne's disguise is revealed, she slaps Figaro twice before beating him; this makes the audience laugh because it is so unexpected.

- **Misunderstandings.** Act 5 is filled with misunderstandings. The fact that Rosine has dressed up as Suzanne and Suzanne has dressed up as Rosine leads to a number of humorous mistakes. Disguise is a classic feature of comedy and adds to the humour because it sees the characters wearing clothes that do not suit them.

The more innovative comic elements include the role played by the scenery, which changes with each act: a room with a sick chair in Act 1; another, more luxurious room for the Countess in Act 2; a courtroom in Act 3; a gallery in Act 4; and the castle's gardens in Act 5. The scenery contributes to the comic aspect of the play's episodes: for example, in Act 1 Chérubin hides underneath the chair before leaping out of the window to avoid being caught.

THE THEME OF LOVE

As its title suggests, love is central to the play, which depicts a number of different romantic relationships:

- Figaro and Suzanne's love is entirely sincere. Apart from Figaro's short-lived misapprehension that Suzanne is unfaithful to him, nothing can shake their feelings for one another. Neither of them needs to resort to deceit or manipulation to win the other over.
- Chérubin is hopelessly in love with Rosine and pours all his energy into trying to charm her. He sings about her and steals one of her ribbons, which he treasures. His love for her is accompanied by passionate adolescent lust.
- After using his cunning to marry Rosine, Almaviva attempts to embark on an affair with Suzanne. This results in the play's only love triangle.

The plot is driven by the characters' romantic feelings, which result in a number of plot twists and comic scenes.

FIGARO'S MONOLOGUE

Figaro's monologue in Act 5, Scene III, in which he discusses his situation and preoccupations at length, is one of the most famous passages in French theatre. At this point in the play, he believes that Suzanne prefers Count Almaviva to him and is worried that his wedding will not go ahead. His jealousy and unhappiness lead him to describe his entire life story, with the aim of showing that he is infinitely more deserving than his presumed rival.

The text revolves around two key themes: love and social circumstances. During this monologue, Figaro utters one of the most famous lines in the play as he attacks the fact that the Count did not attain his social position through his own merit: "[you] [p]ut yourself to the trouble of being born – nothing more!". His romantic disappointment therefore exacerbates the pain he feels at the vast gulf between him and Almaviva, which is largely due to their diametrically opposed social origins.

Figaro's speech is one of the longest monologues in the history of theatre, and is especially remarkable when we consider the time period the play was written in, as such extensive soliloquys were even rarer then than they are today. The monologue is extremely dense and discusses a number of Figaro's worries:

- The monologue begins and ends with his concerns about Suzanne's supposed betrayal.
- He evokes the abject poverty he has found himself in on multiple occasions, which he sees as particularly unfair as he is an honest man. He was raised by bandits and tried to distance himself from them by getting an education, but when this proved to be out of his reach he turned to the theatre. He has experienced a lot and held many jobs, but in the end working as a valet is the only thing that provides him with some measure of stability.
- In the second half of the monologue, he claims that the powerful often resort to theft, which serves to bolster their position. Figaro was raised in an environment where theft was common, but when he tried to leave it behind him he realised that he could only make a living by resorting to deceit and cunning. He believes that he is the victim of the worst kind of theft,

as Almaviva is trying to take his fiancée away from him.

- Finally, he expresses disgust at the differences between him and Almaviva, which are solely due to their social origins. Figaro has to fight for the same privileges that Almaviva has always enjoyed solely by virtue of his birth, but he still does not manage to attain them, even in his personal relationships (as he believes that Suzanne has been unfaithful to him).

In this way, Beaumarchais condemns some aspects of 18th-century society, but the situation he depicts seems hopeless, with the nobility and their unearned privileges on the one hand, and the ordinary people who are embittered because they cannot access the same privileges no matter how hard they work on the other hand. The monologue's controversial political dimension makes it, and the play as a whole, a landmark in Beaumarchais' work.

FURTHER REFLECTION

- In what ways is Figaro's monologue in Act 5, Scene III representative of the play as a whole?
- Comment on Figaro's retort to Almaviva that "[you] [p]ut yourself to the trouble of being born – nothing more!".
- In what ways is Figaro different from the valets depicted in comedies by Molière (French playwright, 1622-1673) and Marivaux (French writer, 1688-1763)? What makes him original?
- *The Marriage of Figaro* serves as the sequel to *The Barber of Seville.* Do you think that the characters have developed between the two plays? Use examples to illustrate your answer.
- *The Marriage of Figaro* is a comedy, which means that its aim is to make the audience laugh. What comic techniques does Beaumarchais use?
- Why could it be said that the play foreshadowed the French Revolution in 1789?

- Comment on the following quotation from the play: "unless there is liberty to criticize, praise has no value" (Act 5, Scene III).
- *The Marriage of Figaro* was censored during the Nazi occupation of France (1940-1944). Which passages do you think were suppressed and why?
- Do you think that Beaumarchais was a misogynist or a defender of women? Justify your answer.

We want to hear from you!
Leave a comment on your online library
and share your favourite books on social media!

FURTHER READING

REFERENCE EDITION

- Beaumarchais, P.-A. (1964) *The Barber of Seville and The Marriage of Figaro*. Trans. Wood, J. London: Penguin.

REFERENCE STUDIES

- Ehrndal, N. (2007) Femmes, révolution et effets comiques dans *Le Mariage de Figaro* de Beaumarchais. *Europeana Collections*. [Online]. [Accessed 27 August 2018]. Available from: <https://www.europeana.eu/portal/en/record/9200111/BibliographicResource_1000085949593.html>

- (No date) Le Mariage de Figaro. *Mount Holyoke*. [Online]. [Accessed 27 August 2018]. Available from: <https://www.mtholyoke.edu/courses/nvaget/331sp08/lemariage.html>

- Skenazene, I. (No date) Les divers aspects du comique dans *Le Mariage de Figaro* : convention et innovation. *Academia.edu*. [Online]. [Accessed 27 August 2018]. Available from: <http://www.academia.edu/24724077/LES_DIVERS_ASPECTS_DU_COMIQUE_DANS_LE_MARIAGE_DE_FIGARO_CONVENTION_ET_INNOVATION>

ADAPTATIONS

- *The Marriage of Figaro*. (1786) [Opera]. Wolfgang Amadeus Mozart. Vienna.

- *Beaumarchais the Scoundrel*. (1996) [Film]. Édouard Molinaro. Dir. France: Téléma, StudioCanal, France 2 Cinéma, France 3 Cinéma.

MORE FROM BRIGHTSUMMARIES.COM

- Reading guide – *The Barber of Seville* by Beaumarchais.

www.brightsummaries.com

Ebook EAN: 9782808011617

Paperback EAN: 9782808011624

Legal Deposit: D/2018/12603/333

This guide was written with the collaboration of Lucile Lhoste for the sections "Royal censorship", "Comic techniques in *The Marriage of Figaro*", "The theme of love" and "Figaro's monologue", and for the box "The relationship between *The Marriage of Figaro* and *The Barber of Seville*".

Cover: © Primento

Digital conception by Primento, the digital partner of publishers.